NEW: First Steps For New Christ-Followers
© 2012 by Andy Blanks. All rights reserved.

Published by youth**ministry**360 in the United States of America.

ISBN 13: 978-1-935832-21-8
ISBN 10: 1935832212

Any reference within this book to Internet addresses of web sites not under the administration of youth**ministry**360 is not to be taken as an endorsement of these web sites by youth**ministry**360. youth**ministry**360 does not vouch for their content nor does youth**ministry**360 make any statement to their functionality.

The "NIV" and "New International Version" trademarks are registered in the United States Patent and Trademark Office by Biblica. Use of either trademark requires the permission of Biblica.

Scripture marked MSG taken from The Message. Copyright © 1993, 1994, 1995, 1996, 2000, 2001, 2002. Used by permission of NavPress Publishing Group.

Design and Layout: Upper Air Creative
Copy Editor: Lynn Groom

FIRST STEPS FOR NEW CHRIST-FOLLOWERS >>>

BY ANDY BLANKS

Published by youth**ministry**360

TABLE OF CONTENTS

NEW WEEK 3: WHAT IT MEANS TO FOLLOW

NEW WEEK 4: LIVING THE NEW LIFE

MORE NEW STUFF

HOW *NEW* WORKS

NEW isn't just another book. It's a highly interactive, super creative, in-depth journey into your NEW life.

Because of this, we thought we needed to take a second and tell you a few things about this book and how it works.

NEW IS A JOURNEY

The concepts in *NEW* build on each other. The book is laid out over four weeks, each week having a mix of different activities to help guide you in understanding this new life you've discovered. *Or that discovered you . . .* Start at the beginning and move from day-to-day, letting each day, and each week, speak to you.

GO AT YOUR OWN SPEED

You might be working through this with other teenagers and an adult leader. If so, you probably want to stay on track. But if you're not, take *NEW* at your own speed. For most of you, this will all be pretty, well, <u>new</u>! Take it slow and soak it in. If you need more than four weeks to work through the book, so be it!

LET EACH DAY BE WHAT IT IS

We didn't make this book a cookie-cutter template where every day is the same. Your life doesn't work that way. Why should this book? Each day is a little different. Some have instructions for stuff to do, some just have a phrase or a verse for you to think about. Take each day of this journal for what it is. (Not bad advice for life, either!)

MAKE SURE YOU HOLD ON TO NEW

The things you will be learning will stick with you forever. But you might want to check back in this book to see what your first steps as a NEW Christ-follower looked like. Plus, this book is slammed full of awesome resources you'll want to use even when you're not such a NEW follower. So, hang on to it!

HOW *NEW* WORKS FOR YOUTH WORKERS OR OTHER ADULTS

If you're a youth worker or another adult, and you've picked up this book for your student (or students), you need to know that *NEW* functions two ways:

STAND-ALONE DEVOTIONAL

This book works perfectly as a stand-alone devotional book. You don't have to do anything in order for your student(s) to engage with this awesome resource. There are four weeks of daily content plus some articles and other stuff, all designed for a teenager to walk through without an adult leader. (Though we absolutely suggest engaging where you can and allowing yourself to be available for questions!)

4-LESSON SMALL GROUP OPTION

However, if you want, you can use *NEW* as the "out of class" piece for a four-session Small Group Bible study meeting. How? Easy. All you have to do is go to http://youthministry360.com/new-believers-small-group-lesson-plans. There you will find a FREE download that enables you to lead a four-session Bible study centered around what your students are learning in *NEW*.

THE NEW YOU: AN INTRODUCTION

If you're holding this book, chances are it's because you've recently taken the first steps on a journey.

You will no doubt respond to the last sentence one of two ways . . .

Some of you reading this right now realize that you are indeed on a journey. You have a good idea of what's up ahead. You can't wait to really get started. If this describes you . . . well, that's pretty cool.

Buckle up. The ride is a wild one!

Others of you will read that first sentence up there and be uneasy. You may be saying to yourself, "I didn't sign up for a journey!" It's OK, though. On many of life's biggest adventures we don't really know we're on one until the trip is already underway.

If you're reading this and you're questioning whether or not you're really on a journey of some sort, an adventure, make no mistake about it: **You are.** You've started something. Something big. Something awesome.

If you're unsure of exactly what you signed up for, it's actually not a bad place to be. After all, you took the first step. A step forward. A step toward something. A step toward Someone.

Whether or not you had a full picture of what your future looked like, you still took a step toward Christ, toward God. What motivated you to do this? Only you know.

BUT FOR WHATEVER REASON, YOU REACHED OUT FOR CHRIST.

MAYBE YOU DOUBTED AND WERE SIMPLY GIVING JESUS A CHANCE TO WIN YOU OVER.

MAYBE YOU TRULY SAW HOW BROKEN AND NEEDY YOU **REALLY ARE.**

OR MAYBE YOU SIMPLY HEARD AND BELIEVED.

MAYBE YOU FELT THAT YOUR LIFE WAS MEANT FOR A GREATER PURPOSE.

Whatever the motivation was, something moved you to consider. To be open. Somewhere along the way, God's very Spirit came alongside you to help you finally choose God over *you*. However it exactly happened, it started you down this path. And what a path it is . . .

YOU SEE, THIS NEW PATH YOU'VE STARTED DOWN IS A PATH OF DISCOVERY. AND WHAT YOU'LL DISCOVER IS WHAT MAKES ALL THE DIFFERENCE.

This path doesn't just lead you to a new label. It doesn't just lead you to a new group of friends. It doesn't just lead you to the "right" and "wrong" way to think, or act, or be.

This path? It starts with God. And it leads to God. And all along the way, you're encountering God. The path is all about God.

Whatever you may have thought before this moment, hear me say this: this path you're on will never, ever lead you to a cleaner, better, happier version of "you." (Take it from someone who's been on the path for a while, this fact becomes more comforting the longer you're on this journey.)

You see, the beginning of your **NEW** journey can't lead to a *better* you. *"Why,"* you ask? Because this journey began with another journey's end. An old journey. A hopeless journey where all of your energy and vision was focused on you. **The old you.**

THIS NEW JOURNEY IS LEADING YOU TO DISCOVER THE NEW YOU.

The moment you truly believed, the moment you handed the leadership of your life to God, the moment you realized you had a HUMONGOUS problem only Jesus could solve . . . in that moment God created something NEW and beautiful out of the ashes of the old, dead you.

AND THE NEW YOU IS SO UNBELIEVABLY INCREDIBLE IT'S ALMOST IMPOSSIBLE TO WRAP YOUR BRAIN AROUND.

The Bible says this about you . . .

IF ANYONE IS IN CHRIST, HE IS A NEW CREATION; THE OLD HAS GONE, THE NEW HAS COME!

BEFORE YOU GAVE YOUR LIFE TO CHRIST, YOU WERE DEAD BECAUSE OF YOUR SINS. BUT THROUGH CHRIST, GOD GAVE YOU LIFE.

The Bible says:

YOU WERE DEAD IN YOUR TRANSGRESSIONS AND SINS ... BUT BECAUSE OF HIS GREAT LOVE FOR US, GOD ... MADE US ALIVE WITH CHRIST.

Your sin would've stood between you and God forever. But Jesus took it away.

Jesus gave you a NEW relationship with God. A NEW purpose. A NEW way of seeing things.

Your mind is NEW. Your heart is NEW. Even your very identity is NEW.

YOU MAY BE SLIGHTLY OVERWHELMED BY ALL OF THIS.

Don't Be.

REMEMBER, I SAID IT WAS A JOURNEY. YOU DON'T HAVE TO KNOW IT ALL TODAY. PART OF BEING NEW IS THAT YOU'RE AN "ALL-AT-ONCE" NEW CREATION IN GOD'S EYES. THE OTHER PART IS THAT YOU'LL SPEND YOUR LIFE ON THIS EARTH **BEING MADE NEW**. GOD WILL ALWAYS BE WORKING IN YOU TO HELP YOU BECOME MORE LIKE HIM. WHICH IS AWESOME.

Sounds pretty amazing, doesn't it?

YOU PROBABLY HAVE LOTS OF QUESTIONS. BUT DON'T WORRY. THAT ONLY MAKES YOU NORMAL. THIS BOOK WILL HELP. IN FACT, THIS BOOK IS ALL ABOUT HELPING!

THE COOL THING IS THAT GOD HAS MADE IT SO THE NEW YOU CAN BEGIN TO SLOWLY BUT SURELY GRASP WHAT THIS NEW LIFE IS ALL ABOUT. HE'S YOUR GUIDE ALONG THE WAY. YOU'RE NEVER ALONE. YOU DON'T EVER HAVE TO FIGURE ANYTHING OUT BY YOURSELF. GOD HAS GIVEN YOU HIMSELF TO SERVE AS A CONSTANT COMPANION.

EVERY JOURNEY STARTS WITH A FEW SMALL STEPS. YOU'VE ALREADY MADE THE MOST IMPORTANT ONES.

If you're ready to keep moving forward, turn the page.

WEEK 1 PREVIEW

"Drivers, start your engines!"

I'm not a NASCAR fan but I've had the chance to go to a race before. And it was a pretty awesome experience.

When the drivers are waiting at the starting line, the excitement of the crowd feels almost physical, like you could reach out and touch it. The noise from the engines rumbles in your stomach no matter how far away you are from the cars. And when they begin to make their way around the track, slow at first, then faster than anything you've ever seen . . . well, even a non-fan like me understands why people love their races.

Think of yourself like a racecar at the starting line. While this book isn't a race, it is an exciting time of growing closer to God. And you're about ready to take off!

START YOUR ENGINE AND GET READY FOR A FUN FEW WEEKS OF LEARNING MORE ABOUT THE NEW LIFE YOU HAVE IN CHRIST.

HERE'S A LOOK AT WHAT TO EXPECT THIS WEEK:

Week 1, Day 1: A devotion on why you need a new life

Week 1, Day 2: An activity to guide you in thinking about your new life

Week 1, Day 3: Thinking about your relationship with God

Week 1, Day 4: An interactive activity about your new purpose

Week 1, Day 5: A devotion on the "know-ability" of God

Week 1, Day 6: An encouragement to rest a little . . .

WEEK 1, DAY 1

This week we're going to talk a little more about the ins and outs of your NEW life and what it really means. So, let's just start at the beginning, shall we?

Why do you need new life anyway? It's an important question to ask, right?

You need new life because without it, you're dead. Seriously. See, when God created the world and everything in it (a narrative you can read in Genesis 1-2), He made Adam and Eve to be perfect. After all, God is perfect. And He wanted man and woman to be able to hang out with Him. Which meant they had to be perfect, too. The only problem was that they broke God's trust. *They became not-perfect.*

Adam and Eve rebelled against the Creator. (You can read all about that in Genesis 3.) The Bible calls this sin. And rebellion against God earned Adam and Eve separation from God and eventual death.

Here's the worst part: From that moment on, every person ever born carried Adam and Eve's sinful heart in them. And that means they carried death with them. That means you, me, the best person you know . . . everyone who has ever rebelled against God earns death.

A really awesome guy named Paul (you can read about him on page 96) wrote a letter to the Romans that says this: "For the wages of sin is death" (Rom. 6:23). Just like when you have a job and your work earns you a wage ("wage" is another word for money), our sin actually earns the wage of death for us.

Not cool, right?

BUT HERE'S THE COOL THING . . .

The rest of that verse from Romans brings a ton of hope to the scene, hope that you already know about: "For the wages of sin is death, **but the gift of God is eternal life in Christ Jesus our Lord**" (emphasis added).

Because Jesus was God's Son, He was perfect. He was the only person in the position to substitute His life for yours. Because God loves you so much, He wanted to make a way to give you life. So God allowed Jesus' death to count in your place:

> God made him who had no sin to be sin for us, so that in him we might become the righteousness of God (2 Cor. 5:21).

By dying on the cross and coming back to life on the third day, Jesus paid the wage of death that your sin rightfully earned you. In other words, Jesus bought you life! You're alive only because of Jesus' sacrifice. Jesus once said,

> "I tell you the truth, whoever hears my word and believes him who sent me has eternal life and will not be condemned; he has crossed over from death to life" (John 5:24).

You could never have been good enough or tried hard enough to save yourself. Your sin would've always kept you separated from God. But Jesus took care of that. And by accepting His sacrifice on your behalf, you have gained life.

You were once dead. But now, and forevermore, YOU ARE ALIVE!

Consider taking a moment to talk to God in prayer about this. *Seriously.* **Don't skip over this. Do it.**
- Thank God that He loves you so, so much!
- Thank God that He had a plan to allow you to escape the death your sin earned you.
- Ask God to remind you how your NEW life can be used to help other people learn how they can cross over from death to life.

WEEK 1, DAY 2

In John 14:6, Jesus said these words: "I am the way and the truth and the life. No one comes to the Father except through me." Jesus said, I am **THE** life! This is what we talked about yesterday. **Jesus is truth.** And by following Him, you have life. A rich, full life today. And a life forever with God.

Today's activity is a simple one: *As much as you can, think about what it means to have this NEW life.*

Ask yourself these questions and really contemplate the answers:
• How does having this new life with God make you feel?
• What is different *right now* about this new life?
• Can you describe the way you look at Jesus now? Is it different than before?
• Has this new life changed the way you see others? How?
• Have you really thought about what led you to turn to God? If not, think about that today.

If you want, use this page to write down your thoughts. If you have a journal or a blog, maybe you could write them down there. Or, if you're not the "writing type," simply think about them as you go through your day.

WEEK 1, DAY 3

Relationships. They're full of drama, right? Without Jesus, our relationship with God would have more drama than you can imagine.

Go to Romans 5 in your Bible. Take a second and read verses 6-10. (Read them twice if you need to.) Let's take verses 6-8 first. Here Paul was saying that maybe, just maybe, someone might occasionally sacrifice his or her life for a great person. But verse 8 says something entirely different: Jesus died for us while we were stuck in our sin. (In other words, we weren't very great at all.) Now let's look at 9-10. Verse 9 uses a big word. **It says we've been justified.** *Justified* is a legal term meaning that we were guilty, but we've been declared innocent. Through the blood Jesus shed on the cross for you, your guilt was wiped away.

But look what verse 10 says about what we were: enemies! Apart from Christ, we were God's enemies! Ouch! But verse 10 uses another big but important word: reconciled. *Reconciled* means to restore. To bring back together. **We were God's enemies.** Paul spoke to this again in Colossians 1:21: Once you were alienated from God and were enemies in your minds because of your evil behavior.

But Jesus' payment for our sins brought us back together with God. Without Jesus, you wouldn't be able to know God. You wouldn't be able to be close to Him. You'd be His enemy. Jesus restored your relationship with God. *This new relationship?* It's a *huge* part of your NEW life.

Think about how you would answer these questions:
• What part of this new relationship with God are you enjoying the most?
• What has been the biggest surprise for you in enjoying a new closeness with God?
• How is this relationship changing who you are?

WEEK 1, DAY 4

WHEN GOD GIVES US NEW LIFE, HE GIVES US A NEW PURPOSE.

What do I mean by purpose? Basically, your purpose is the reason why you're alive. It's the goal of all your energy, thoughts, and actions. And when God gave you a new life, your purpose, like everything else in your life, became God-centered.

What is your new purpose? It's interesting. It can actually look a few different ways. It could look like Jesus' words to His disciples in Matthew 28:19: *"Therefore go and make disciples of all nations, baptizing them in the name of the Father and of the Son and of the Holy Spirit."*

Or, from Paul's words to the Corinthians in 2 Corinthians 5:18: *All this is from God, who reconciled us to himself through Christ and gave us the ministry of reconciliation.* Or from the prophet Micah's words in Micah 6:8: *And what does the LORD require of you? To act justly and to love mercy and to walk humbly with your God.* Or from John's words in 1 John 4:11: *Dear friends, since God so loved us, we also ought to love one another.*

The answer is that each of these verses and many more speak to your NEW purpose. You have a new purpose, a new reason for living, a new object of your dreams and plans. You have a new lens through which to view your present and future.

On the following page, you'll see three categories. "High School" represents your present. "College" represents your near future. And "Career" represents a distant future. Take a moment to reflect on how your NEW purpose changes the way you look at these three categories of your life.

How does your new life with Christ change the way you see your present, your immediate future, and your life as an adult?

High School   College   Career

WEEK 1, DAY 5

Can you imagine what it would be like to have a best friend you didn't know? *That sentence doesn't even make sense, does it?* The very idea of having a best friend means sharing life with him or her. You know your best friend. If you didn't, he or she wouldn't be your best friend. Imagine someone saying to you, "My best friend and I have never met. I'm not even sure what she likes and what she doesn't. But, we're BFF for sure!" You'd look at that person like she were nuts, wouldn't you?

And yet people all over this world have a similar kind of relationship with the "god" they serve. These people devote their lives to gods they don't know. To put it better, they serve gods they can't know because they don't exist. *Should we look at them like they're nuts, too?* I don't think so. If you ask me, I think we should have two responses . . .

1. We should be thankful we serve the one, true God, and that we can know Him! We serve the God who revealed Himself over and over again to real people. These accounts are recorded in the Bible. We should be thankful God chose to go a step further and send His Son to live on this earth. He intersected with real people, too, both friends and enemies who testified in writing that He actually lived and walked on this earth. And we should be thankful God has sent His Spirit to live within each one of us, assuring us of His presence, and reminding us that He is real.

2. Our hearts should break. The men, women, and teenagers all over the world who give their lives worshiping statues, myths, or philosophies are basically good people. Like you and me. They believe in what they are doing. But in the end, the thing they serve isn't "knowable" like God is. And that's a pretty tragic thing.

One of the greatest gifts God ever gave us was the Bible, a historically validated account of His interactions with real people. **What an amazing thing it is to be able to know the one we serve.** Our Lord. Our friend!

TAKE A SECOND AND THINK ABOUT THESE QUESTIONS IN LIGHT OF WHAT YOU JUST READ.

1. Thousands of years ago, God spoke through the prophet Jeremiah, predicting the relationship He currently has with us. God said we'd be able to truly know Him in our hearts and minds (Jer. 31:33-34). **The Bible is the main way we get to know God.** Describe your attitude toward reading the Bible. Do you enjoy it? Does it overwhelm you? Do you feel closer to God when you read it?

2. The Apostle Paul wrote that people can clearly see evidence of God and His characteristics in the natural world around them (Rom. 1:19-20). **Where do you see this at work in your life?** Describe how seeing God in creation helps you know God.

3. Because God is real, David could say this about Him: "The Lord is near to all who call on him" (Ps. 145:18). **When have you felt God close to you?** Describe how this nearness helps you know God.

WEEK 1, DAY 6

RELAX ...

YOU'VE COVERED A LOT THIS WEEK. AND THE JOURNEY ONLY GETS BETTER AS YOU GO ALONG. TAKE A BREAK. REST. REFLECT ON SOME OF WHAT YOU'VE LEARNED ABOUT YOUR NEW LIFE. AND GO OUT TODAY AND ENJOY IT ...

WEEK 1 ROUND UP

We started this week with the goal of trying to understand a little more about the ins and outs of this NEW life you have in Christ. Hopefully you were able to take the chance to really think about what this life means for your life today and down the road.

Of course, there is so much more to it than what we were able to cover in these few short pages. Hopefully, though, you were at least able to lay a good foundation to start building on.

And that's really what this first week of this journal was: a foundation. The first week sets the stage for the remaining three weeks. **So, get ready. You're about to get into some even cooler stuff.** Get ready to begin learning about God and what makes Him so awesome, what it means to follow Jesus, and what living the NEW life looks like in the real world.

What are you waiting on? Keep those pages turning. The start of Week 2 is just a few pages away. (But in the meantime, take a moment when you're free and read a pretty cool little article on pages 30 and 31 about *why* and *how* to study your Bible.)

HOW TO READ THE BIBLE

This is the first of three short articles you can read whenever you have time. Each of the articles unpacks one aspect of your NEW life. This one is all about how to study the Bible.

The Bible is the living and active Word of God. Engaging with your Bible with the purpose of encountering God and growing closer to Christ is the key to powerful life change. But knowing how to approach the Bible can be tricky. So, I want to pass along two helpful strategies for interacting with the Bible. Try them out and see what you think. (And if you want more strategies, turn to page 100.)

STRATEGY 1: MEDITATING ON SCRIPTURE

No, not *meditating* like a yoga instructor or a ninja or something. Meditating on God's Word is simply when you read it and think about it. Let's practice a bit . . .

STEP 1 Clear your thoughts. Pray that the Holy Spirit will help you see God's truth in this passage. *Turn in your Bible to Psalm 100.*

STEP 2 Read the psalm slowly. Read it again, focusing on each word.

STEP 3 Clear your head of any distractions. Now read the verses one last time, looking for words or ideas that jump out at you. You may choose to circle these words or phrases, or write them in a journal.

Now finish up:
• Think about how these verses make you feel. What do you want to say to God after reading this?
• Think about how these verses might change your outlook on your day or your life.
• Pray to God thanking Him for what He has shown you through His Word.

Simple enough, right? You can use this is a guide to meditate on any passage of Scripture.

STRATEGY 1: MINING SCRIPTURE

Meditating on God's Word is important. But *mining* is, too. Mining is searching the depths of God's Word for a greater understanding of specific passages. Let's give it a shot.

STEP 1: Read the passage.
- *Let's read Galatians 6:1-5.*
- Read it again, paying attention to what stands out as important.
- Write down any words you think are important, or any questions you have after reading the passage.

_____

_____

_____

(NOTE: If you have questions, now is the time to answer them. Search for key words in the concordance in the back of your Bible. Or ask your parents, youth worker, or another adult you trust.)

STEP 2: Know the context.
- Go back a few verses before the passage you're studying. Read until you come to your passage.
- Now read a few verses past your passage. You should have a better idea of what's going on now.

STEP 3: Find the main idea.
- Write what you think is the main idea for Galatians 6:1-5.

_____

_____

STEP 4: Live the truth.
- The Bible must influence your life. Come up with a few ways you could apply the main truth of the passage to your life.

Two cool strategies. Put both of them to use and watch yourself grow closer to the Lord.

A NEW Perspective . . . .

"What a God we have! And how fortunate we are to have him, this Father of our Master Jesus! Because Jesus was raised from the dead, we've been given a brand-new life and have everything to live for, including a future in heaven—and the future starts now!"
1 Peter 1:3-4 (MSG)

WEEK 2 PREVIEW

Chances are, if you're reading this book you may be pretty new to this faith thing. Over the years I've seen tons of teenagers in your exact same shoes. **The excitement and freshness of NEW faith is so encouraging to me.** It never gets old. But I've also seen something happen in people as they move along in life. I've seen their faith grow stale.

Why does this happen? A lot of reasons, I guess. But I think there's one common explanation for why people's faith doesn't grow as they grow: *I think many people take their eyes off God.* Their faith becomes about rules and "being good," or about their own efforts, when it was really supposed to be about knowing, loving, and following God. Faith doesn't work any other way.

This second week of NEW is all about getting to know God more. My prayer for you is that you would realize this week how awesome it is to know God (to really know Him!) and to see your life transformed as a result.

HERE'S A LOOK AT WHAT TO EXPECT THIS WEEK:

Week 2, Day 1: An interactive look at God's attributes

Week 2, Day 2: A creative look at God's love

Week 2, Day 3: A devotion/Bible study on God as judge

Week 2, Day 4: A challenge to dwell on God's holiness

Week 2, Day 5: A look at God's forgiveness

Week 2, Day 6: Getting creative in your praise

WEEK 2, DAY 1

In your mind, picture the person or people who are primarily responsible for taking care of you. Maybe it's a mom or dad. Maybe it's a grandparent. Maybe it's a foster mom or dad. Whomever it is, picture them. Now, in the space below, describe them in three sentences or so.

OK, now think about how you just described him or her. Did you write about how your dad looks? Did you talk about how generous your grandmom is? Chances are you listed what could probably be described as characteristics or attributes. In most cases, when we think of someone we tend to think of them in terms of their attributes, those aspects of their personality that make them who they are.

Do you know God has attributes too? He most definitely does. See, God isn't some impersonal, unknown, detached force dwelling high above the universe. Over and over again the Bible shows God involving Himself in our lives in ways that reveal a ton about His nature. And as we talked about a few days ago, we can learn all about who God is through the way the Bible speaks of His attributes.

Let's do a little exercise to help you know a little more about who God is . . .

HOW DOES THE BIBLE DESCRIBE GOD?

Below you'll find a list of verses that speak to one or more of God's attributes. Take a minute and look up some (or all) of the verses. In the blanks beside each verse reference, write down the attribute(s) the verse mentions. I've done the first one for you:

Psalm 85:7   _LOVE_____

Psalm 145:9   _____

John 1:14   _____

Deuteronomy 32:4   _____

Luke 1:49   _____

2 Corinthians 12:9   _____

1 John 1:9   _____

Psalm 11:7   _____

Job 5:9   _____

OK, SO YOU'VE JUST LOOKED AT SOME OF GOD'S ATTRIBUTES. NOW WHAT?

So, this God who has called you to this NEW life? The one who made a way for you to be in perfect relationship with Him? These attributes are a picture of who He is! When you pray to Him, this is who you're praying to. When you call on Him, this is who answers you. He is real. And He acts according to His nature. **God's attributes help us know exactly who it is we love and serve.**

Most of the days in this journal have a specific takeaway or application. The takeaway on this day is simply to think about God and all His amazing attributes. _Let this knowledge be the ground floor for the rest of this week spent digging deeper into exactly who God is._

WEEK 2, DAY 2

Of all God's attributes, His love may be the one that speaks to us the most. After all, His love motivates all that He's done for us and for the world. These pages are a collection of verses about God's love. **For today, choose one of these verses and memorize it.** Keep it in your heart and mind as you go through your day and your week.

Jesus replied, "If anyone loves me, he will obey my teaching. My Father **WILL LOVE HIM**, and we will come to him and make our home with him." —John 14:23

BUT GOD DEMONSTRATES HIS OWN LOVE FOR US IN THIS: WHILE WE WERE STILL SINNERS, CHRIST DIED FOR US. ROMANS 5:8

Whoever does not love does not know God, because **GOD IS LOVE**. —1 John 4:8

For God **SO LOVED THE WORLD** that he gave his one and only Son, that whoever believes in him shall not perish but have eternal life.—John 3:16

The LORD detests the way of the wicked but **HE LOVES** those who pursue righteousness.—Proverbs 15:9

But because of his **GREAT LOVE FOR US**, God, who is rich in mercy made us alive with Christ even when we were dead in transgressions—it is by grace you have been saved.—Ephesians 2:4-5

This is love: not that we loved God, but that **HE LOVED US** and sent his Son as an atoning sacrifice for our sins.—1 John 4:10

Because **YOUR LOVE** is better than life, my lips will glorify you.—Psalm 63:3

This is how God **SHOWED HIS LOVE** among us: He sent his one and only Son into the world that we might live through him.—1 John 4:9

How **GREAT IS THE LOVE** the Father has **LAVISHED ON US**, that we should be called children of God! And that is what we are!—1 John 3:1

For great is **YOUR LOVE** toward me; you have delivered me from the depths of the grave.—Psalms 86:13

And so we know and rely on the love God has for us. **GOD IS LOVE**. Whoever lives in love lives in God, and God in him.—1 John 4:16

A new command I give you: Love one another. **AS I HAVE LOVED YOU**, so you must love one another. By this all men will know that you are my disciples, if you love one another.—John 13:34

YOUR LOVE, O LORD, reaches to the heavens, your faithfulness to the skies.—Psalms 36:5

Neither height nor depth, nor anything else in all creation, will be able to separate us from the **LOVE OF GOD** that is in Christ Jesus our Lord.—Romans 8:39

WEEK 2, DAY 3

Have you ever heard anyone say anything about God similar to the following phrases?

"God is just."

"God is the righteous judge."

Whether or not you've heard God described in this way, it's important to understand this part of God's character. Take a second and write what you think it means that God is just, or that He is a righteous judge.

Did you have a hard time defining that phrase? No worries if it was tough. We're about to dig-in to it right now. But here's a warning: this is one of those parts of God's character that can make us squirm a bit . . .

Let's jump in. Read Psalm 7:11. Now read Nahum 1:3. (Yikes!) Write down how it makes you feel to read these verses. How does it feel seeing God described this way?

Simply put, we'd much rather camp out on God's love and mercy. We don't like to think of God as angry or full of wrath. We don't like to think of Him as judge. But once we understand this concept, we actually should come to a place where we want to see God as the righteous judge! Let me explain.

Deuteronomy 32:4 says about God, "He is the Rock, his works are perfect, and all his ways are just. A faithful God who does no wrong, upright and just is he." Look in the first part of the verse. Circle the word that describes God's works. How are they described? That's right. **Perfect.**

God's perfection is the key to understanding and appreciating His judgment.

So, we serve a God who is perfect. Perfectly perfect. So much so that He is literally incapable of tolerating sin or evil. And so God's way is to drive out all sin. Which is where wrath and judgment and punishment come in.

It's like this: God is the life-giver. Born out of His great love, He chose to create humans. But we rebelled against Him. Heck, we rebel against Him every day. Rebellion = sin. And sin = death. But God doesn't condemn sin and sinners because He's bored or because He needs a hobby. He does it because He's perfect.

His love is perfect. His anger is perfect. His mercy is perfect. His jealousy is perfect. And because He is perfectly good and pure and righteous, He perfectly judges all sin. His judgments and His justice? Yup, they're perfect too.

God isn't like us. His anger isn't emotional, catty, or unfair. His judgment isn't spiteful, uneven, or unpredictable. We need a God who is perfect in all His ways, even the ones that are uncomfortable to us. If He wasn't perfect, He wouldn't be worthy of our devotion. But He is, and so He is.

Think about this:

1. In Romans 5:9, Paul says we've been saved from God's anger and judgment through Jesus' death. Jesus took on your sin. He took on God's perfect anger and judgment that was supposed to be for you and me. How does this make you feel? What do you want to say to Jesus after thinking about this?

2. There's another side to God's justice. Read Psalms 103:6. How does this make you feel about God's justice?

3. Is it tricky to think about God as perfect in His love and compassion and also perfect in His anger and wrath? Why? How is it possible to believe these seemingly opposite truths?

WEEK 2, DAY 4

Of all God's attributes, holiness is one you probably hear referred to a lot. And yet, holiness can be kind of hard to actually define. That's why I love how this quote puts it:

"The holiness of God is the 'Godness' of God. It is what sets him apart from everyone else."—*Vaughan Roberts*

God is "set apart" from everything else! He's different. He's "other." Why? Because of His "Godness"! Now that's pretty cool.

In 1 Peter 1:15-16, Peter encourages us to match Jesus' holiness. Peter says this: "But just as he who called you is holy, so be holy in all you do; for it is written: 'Be holy, because I am holy.'"

There are quite a few ways to think about applying this verse. Today, I want to encourage you to think about following this verse in one specific way.

**As you go through your day, take Peter's words to heart.
In your thoughts, words, and actions, see what it feels like to
try and mimic God's "Godness."**

Be aware of how you're imitating God's attributes of love, peace, compassion, faithfulness, and so on. And take notice of what a difference this focus will make in your life and in the lives of those around you.

WEEK 2, DAY 5

In the early 1990's, a tragedy like few others swept across the African nation of Rwanda. Two different ethnic groups, the Tutsis and the Hutus, had known pretty tense relationships with one another. But in 1994, the tension boiled over. The Hutus murdered over a million Tutsis (along with many other Hutus who were sympathetic to the Tutsis' cause).

People who had lived next to each other for decades suddenly turned on their neighbors. People murdered their in-laws. Their cousins. Their friends. It was a sickening turn of events.

Two decades later, Rwanda is different in part because of a radical explosion of forgiveness and reconciliation. It's too long of a story to tell here. **But amazing healing has happened.** Thanks in part to government trials where people confessed and sought forgiveness, Rwandans are working to put this tragedy behind them. And so it's not uncommon to see a man working next to the man who murdered his family member. *Certainly there is still pain.* And things aren't perfect. But it is a surprising lesson in grace and forgiveness.

The reason this story makes such an impact with us is because it goes against what we feel in our hearts to be a normal or expected reaction.

If you think about it, the forgiveness God offers us is very similar.

Read Ephesians 1:3-8. This is a powerful passage from Paul's letter to the Ephesians. First, let the words of verse 4 sink in. God has chosen you to be blameless. Blameless is another way of saying sinless. *"I'm not sinless,"* you *say.* And you're right. None of us are. What Paul is saying here is that God knew all along that you would accept Christ's payment for your sins. So, in some ways, God forgave you before you even knew it!

Now look at verses 7-8. Remember the God that we read about a few pages back? The one who hates sin? Whose wrath and judgment are awakened by wickedness? Yeah, that God. Well, Paul says here He lavishes you with grace, redeeming you, forgiving your sins. Why? Because you deserve it? Nope. *Because of His amazing grace and love and mercy.* How awesome is that!

Psalm 103:12 says, "As far as the east is from the west, so far has he removed our transgressions from us." Your sins have been wiped clean by God. He chose long ago to make a way for your sin-debt to be paid, but for you to still live. Jesus paid your penalty.

As unexpected and undeserved as it may feel, forgiveness is yours.

Think about this:

1. Do you have any friends who beat themselves up over the mistakes they've made in their lives? What might you say to help them begin to understand the forgiveness God longs to give them?

2. Jesus said in Luke 6:37 that if we want God's forgiveness, we have to be willing to forgive others. Who in your life do you need to forgive? What will it take for you to move in that direction?

3. Do you ever look at yourself and not like what you see? Do you feel guilt or shame because of sin in your past, or sin habits in your present? How does knowing that Jesus gave His life for your forgiveness change the way you see your value and worth?

WEEK 2, DAY 6

Hopefully you've enjoyed learning more about who God is. Today, have some fun. Look at the list of attributes below. **Choose one of God's attributes and create something that praises God for this part of His character.** Take a series of photographs. Write a poem. Paint a painting. Write a song or a short story. Whatever you do, create something that shows God how much you love Him and how thankful you are for your NEW life with Him.

Date : / /   Subject :

COMPASSIONATE
eternal
faithful
POWERFUL
ALL-KNOWING
good
gracious
SOVEREIGN
unchanging
merciful
ALL-POWERFUL
ever-present
RIGHTEOUS

WEEK 2 ROUND UP

GOD IS...

God is awesome, amazing, powerful, wonderful . . . He is all of these things! And this week you've had a chance to begin discovering some of what makes Him who He is. I pray that you had a good experience soaking in some of God's attributes. **Remember, the goal is never to merely collect knowledge or facts.** It's always, *always* about relationship. The goal is for you to know God better so you can stay closer to Him, and watch your life be changed as a result. (Part of staying close to God is communicating with Him in prayer. When you have time, there's a great article on the next page all about how to stay close to God in prayer.)

You're about halfway done with this book. But some of the best stuff is still to come. If you thought learning about God's attributes was cool, you're going to love Week 3!

HOW TO PRAY

This is the second of three short articles you can read whenever you have time. Each of the articles unpacks one aspect of your NEW life. This one is all about how to pray.

Here's an interesting question to consider as you navigate this NEW life in Christ: **Is there a right and wrong way to pray?** Surprisingly, Jesus seems to imply that there is. First let's take a quick look at an example of what Jesus said was a not-so-good way to go about praying.

Read Matthew 6:5-8. Finished? Good. Now, Jesus seems to take issue with the heart behind the prayers being offered by people He called "hypocrites." He spoke out against people who were more concerned with looking super-religious than they were with communicating with God. **That's why Jesus mentioned praying in private.** He wasn't saying it's never OK to pray in public. Jesus' concern was the heart behind the prayer. He went on to say that a ton of words won't help either. God knows what we need. Wasting words to sound smart or seem holy doesn't fool God.

So, Jesus made it clear that God desires prayer that's heartfelt and purely motivated. And in the verses following the ones you just read, Jesus gives a really cool model for how to go about praying to God. *This is often called the Lord's Prayer.* Take a second and read the prayer in Matthew 6:9-13.

Jesus didn't give the Lord's Prayer so that we would only pray one way. In other words, Jesus wasn't saying to copy the words of the prayer. He was simply giving us a model to serve as a guide for our prayers.

On the next page, we'll look at each verse and what it says to us about modeling our own prayers after the Lord's Prayer.

The Lord's Prayer serves as a guide for our own communication with God. Walk through each verse, reading the heading below, and following the prompts to have a meaningful time of prayer with God.

VS. 9: PRAISE GOD The first thing we do when we pray is to praise God. In the space below, tell God He is great. Praise Jesus for His sacrifice. Thank God for His blessings.

VS. 10: OPEN MY EYES God is at work and He's chosen you to be a part of His plan. In the space below, ask God to open your eyes to opportunities where He can use you.

VS. 11: ASK YOUR FATHER God knows what you need. He promises to meet your needs. In the space below, take your needs to God. Trust Him to meet them.

VS. 12: SEEK AND GIVE MERCY If you believe in Christ, your sins are forgiven. Confess your sins to God. Thank Him for forgiving you. Then pray about those you need to forgive.

VS. 13: GIVE ME STRENGTH God promises to give us strength when we're tempted. In the space below, ask God to give you the strength to resist temptation. Thank Him in advance for providing you with His strength.

Before You Finish . . .
One of the most important aspects of praying is listening. As you close your prayer, simply be quiet and reflect on this time. God will speak to you through your thoughts, your circumstances, and His Word. Patiently listen to Him . . .

By praying through the Lord's Prayer, your communication will be right in line with Jesus' ideal model for prayer.

"MY MOUTH WILL SPEAK IN PRAISE OF THE LORD. LET EVERY CREATURE PRAISE HIS HOLY NAME FOR EVER AND EVER."
PSALMS 145:21

A NEW PERSPECTIVE . . .

WEEK 3 PREVIEW

WHAT DOES IT MEAN TO FOLLOW JESUS?

WHAT KIND OF LIFE DOES JESUS CALL YOU TO?

WHAT DOES HE EXPECT?

These questions launch you into a week of looking at Jesus' call to follow Him. And let's just be really clear. **This call to following Jesus is the call to the NEW life you've recently discovered.** The call to be a follower or disciple of Christ isn't some extra special call for *super Christians*. Jesus' call to follow wasn't separated from His offer of salvation.

We know that salvation only comes through faith in Jesus. We can't earn salvation through our actions. *However, our actions are proof of our salvation.* When Christ saves us, He expects us to actively follow Him. That's what being a disciple is all about. And whether you know it or not, you're called to be a disciple. To be a follower.

This week we'll look a lot closer at that call. It's a powerful week so don't take it lightly. But it's also refreshing and uplifting. After all, you get the privilege of knowing God and having a relationship with Him. **What are you waiting on? Let's get started!**

HERE'S A LOOK AT WHAT TO EXPECT THIS WEEK:

Week 3, Day 1: A devotion looking at Jesus as the center of everything

Week 3, Day 2: An interactive look at responding to Jesus' call

Week 3, Day 3: A creative look at Jesus as the ONLY way to life

Week 3, Day 4: A Bible study looking closer at the call to follow Christ

Week 3, Day 5: An interactive look at the story of the rich man

Week 3, Day 6: A gentle reminder to keep Jesus first

WEEK 3, DAY 1

Jesus. In the words of the old hymn, "there's just something about that name."

Jesus demands a response. No one is neutral when it comes to Him. People either love Him and want to talk about Him, or they don't (and they don't). Have you noticed that many people will kindly let you toss around the name "God," but bring Jesus into the conversation, and they get uncomfortable?

It's true: Jesus is kind of a big deal . . .

This isn't a new development. Jesus' role as "lightening rod" is not unique to our culture. Not by a long shot. Jesus has been the hot-button center of cultural conversations since He preached His first sermon. **Jesus is and always has been at the center of everything.** In fact, you could even say that Jesus is the central character of the Bible. Which is an amazing statement, if you think about it. But it goes even further than that!

In his letter to the Colossians, Paul paints an incredible picture of Jesus, maybe the fullest, most powerful picture of Jesus in the Bible. Take a moment and read Paul's words in Colossians 1:15-20. On second thought, you'll probably need to read these verses through a couple of times. So take *two* moments if you need to.

Where do you even start in this amazing description? In verse 15 we learn that in Jesus, we actually are looking at God. How do you think that must have felt to the people reading this in the 1st century who might have actually seen Jesus? *Pretty cool, right?* Verse 16 says that not only was Jesus active in creating the world and everything in it, but that it was created for Him! (Think about that next time you see a beautiful sunrise.) Verse 17 says that without Jesus, all of creation would literally fall apart. *He is the cosmic glue of the universe.* Verses 18-20 are almost too much to handle . . . Jesus is first among all things everywhere, throughout all time. **He is God. Fully God.** And through Him all people have the chance for eternal life.

Whoa . . .

SO HOW DO YOU RESPOND TO THAT?

This rest of this page is yours. Do with it what you wish.
- If right now you're in awe of Jesus, don't do anything on this page. Maybe just sit and reflect.
- If you're bubbling over with praise, don't keep it in: draw a picture or write a note to Jesus expressing what's in your heart.
- If you're confused and a little overwhelmed, look back at the passage and use this space to write down your questions. Arrange to sit down with your youth minister or another adult to talk through them.

Whatever you do, don't do nothing.

Don't move on with your day without allowing yourself to be moved by Jesus Christ, the Son of God.

WEEK 3, DAY 2

When Jesus began to gather the guys who would become His 12 disciples, He didn't give them job descriptions and have them sign contracts. Nope. He went about it another way.

Read Matthew 4:18-20. Jesus looked at these two brothers and said, "Follow Me." The crazy thing? They did! Peter and Andrew might have heard of Jesus, but they couldn't have known the extent of who He was. **So answer this:** Why do you think they followed Him? If you were in their shoes, what questions would you have asked? Would you have followed Jesus? Why or why not? **Answer these questions in the space below.**

Read Matthew 4:21-22. What did James and John leave behind to follow Jesus? (Here's a hint: Not only their father, but their occupation as well.) What have you left behind to follow Jesus? Answer in the space below.

Read Matthew 9:9. Matthew was a tax collector. People saw him as a traitor. But Jesus saw him as valuable. Jesus sees value in you, too. Write down any specific insecurity you may feel about becoming a Christ-follower. Then, pray to God, trusting Him to take you as you are and remake you into a powerful resource for His Kingdom.

IN JOHN 14:6, JESUS SAID . . . I AM

the WAY,

and

the TRUTH,

and

the LIFE.

NO ONE COMES TO **THE** FATHER EXCEPT THROUGH ME.

The world tells you there's more than one way to find God, if there's even a God to find. The world tells you there's no such thing as absolute truth. The world tells you the life you have on this earth, today, is all there is. Better make the most of it! **But Jesus makes it clear:** There is a God, and Jesus is the only way to access Him. There is only one truth, and God is the source of it. *And about your life?* Jesus says real life starts with Him. And it never, ever ends.

So, who do you listen to? The world? Or Jesus? You have to choose. Who will you believe?

WEEK 3, DAY 4

Today you're going to be taking an up close look at the call Jesus gave to anyone who would follow Him. Take a moment and read the passage printed below:

> [24] Then Jesus said to his disciples, "If anyone would come after me, he must deny himself and take up his cross and follow me. [25] For whoever wants to save his life will lose it, but whoever loses his life for me will find it.—Matthew 16:24-25

Two verses. That's it. Two simple verses. But let me assure you, they are quite literally packed with importance. Let's dig in and see exactly what they have to teach us.

First, let's look at the first condition Jesus put on following Him. He said if you want to follow me, you have to "deny yourself." **In your own words, what do you think it means to deny yourself?**

You know, following Jesus is all about power. It's simple really. Do you want the power over your life? Or are you willing to give it over? **Denying yourself = handing over the power.** It comes down to this: who will rule your life? The creator of all life? Or you?

Think for a second about that question. In your opinion, why is denying yourself so vital to following Christ? Why doesn't the alternative work?

NOW HERE'S THE REALLY INTERESTING PART. JESUS WANTS YOU TO TAKE UP YOUR CROSS.

"Huh? Take up my cross? Where am I going to get a cross? And where do I have to take it?"

Jesus isn't being literal. He's using a metaphor. **A word picture.** Let's think about the cross for a second. See, the cross was reserved for the worst criminals. It was a mark of shame. It was a death reserved for the outcasts of society.

Jesus is telling you that following Him means you aren't going to win any popularity contests. Following Jesus won't make you lots of friends. If anything, it may cost you some. Following Jesus puts a mark on you. A mark of somebody who is different than the world.

Answer this: How does being known as a Christ-follower set you at odds with the world around you? What are some examples of how you might face being made fun of, or worse, because you have set yourself apart as a follower of Christ?

How does all of this make you feel? Be honest. Does it seem hard? Does it seem unfair? Do you wish you could believe but not have to be so "out there"?

Here's the truth: If you feel this way, it's not a surprise to Jesus. *You're not the first person to look at the road of discipleship and notice it's kind of bumpy.* But I hope you understand that this is the definition of being a follower. You can't sign up for the easier route.

We sometimes separate faith from action. We tend to act as if we could believe in Jesus, and be saved from our sins, but live an unchanged life. **The problem is that Jesus never gave us that option.** He expects us to follow Him, and to follow Him at a cost. But following Him means life. Abundant life, both here in this world and in Heaven.

I don't know about you, but I want to be a part of that! Don't feel the pressure today to do anything. Just think about all of this. Take it in. Ask God to help you process what you're learning, and to help you see the joy in following Him, even in tough times.

WEEK 3

DAY 5

READ MARK 10: 17-31

Is Jesus saying money is bad? Of course not. What was the problem then? Answer in the next square.

MONEY ISN'T BAD. JESUS JUST KNEW THAT THE MAN'S LOVE FOR MONEY WAS THE ONE THING COMING BETWEEN HIM AND JESUS.

If the man had loved bacon more than Jesus, Jesus would have told him to **GIVE AWAY ALL HIS BACON.**

IF THE MAN HAD LOVED TV MORE THAN JESUS, JESUS WOULD HAVE TOLD HIM TO GIVE AWAY HIS TV.

Here's the question for you ...

What in your life is coming between you and your willingness to follow Jesus? Answer in the following squares.

JESUS KNOWS HE'S **THE BEST THING FOR YOU**. HE WANTS YOU TO FOLLOW HIM. WRITE A PRAYER ASKING JESUS TO HELP YOU GET RID OF THE THINGS KEEPING YOU FROM FOLLOWING HIM MORE.

WEEK 3, DAY 6

Hebrews 6:1 says, "Therefore let us leave the elementary teachings about Christ and go on to maturity . . ." Jesus is at the heart of the NEW you. If you're going to be all Jesus desires you to be, you have to keep growing in your knowledge of Him. **Stay close to Jesus.** Learn more about Him through the Bible. Through prayer. And just through doing life. If you do, you'll grow. *No more baby faith for you!* Your vision will grow. Your heart will grow. And you'll find yourself being used by Christ more and more to make His name known in this world.

WEEK 3, ROUND UP

SO, HOW ARE YOU FEELING RIGHT NOW?

Have the demands of this new life started to sink in yet? Listen, it's OK to admit it: the expectations of living as a Christ-follower can at times seem a bit overwhelming. But that's just our sinful nature talking. What do I mean? Simple. **You were designed to follow.** Before you were even a thought in your mom's mind (even before your mom's, mom's, mom's, mom's mom was a thought in *her* mom's mind) God had His eye on you. He knew that you would one day be born. And that sometime after that, years later, you would realize your total need for Him. **God knew you would reach out and accept the grace and the life He offered through Christ.** Get it? God knew all along you were cut out for this. He knew all along your life would be wrapped up in His. "Following" is your ultimate purpose, the ultimate fulfillment of who you were meant to be. **So don't be overwhelmed.** Don't focus on the fact that it will be tough at times. Be comforted by the fact that God lives. Jesus is who He said He was. You've been chosen to live in Truth. There is great freedom and joy in this. Take heart! **The call to follow equals life.**

Get ready for the final week of NEW, a really practical snapshot of what it looks like to live as a follower in your everyday world.

You're going to love it!

TALKING ABOUT THE NEW YOU

This is the last of three short articles you can read whenever you have time. Each of the articles unpacks one aspect of your NEW life. This one is all about how to talk about your NEW life.

"If you died tonight, where would you spend eternity?"

There's a good chance your parent or guardian had someone they didn't know walk up to them and ask them this question when they were teenagers. (Maybe you've had someone walk up to you and ask the same one.) **It's not a bad question.** In fact, it's a great question. In many ways it's the *right question*. It's not that the question is wrong or outdated. **It's just that our culture has changed.**

You see, there was a time in our country where culture was much more accepting of this type of approach to talking about faith. But people (who are a lot smarter than me) have noted big shifts over the last 10 or 20 years when it comes to this model of engaging in faith conversations. And according to them, this type of engagement is not as effective as it once was.

It's not that faith has changed. God is timeless. It's that society has changed. And if you want to be able to have meaningful chats with friends, or strangers, about your NEW life in Christ, older approaches may not be as effective. **And we should all want to be as effective as possible at sharing our awesome news.**

That's what this article is for: to help you talk about your NEW faith. My goal with this short article isn't really to give you techniques or strategies. I just want to help you think about how you'll approach the important conversations regarding what's happened in your life.

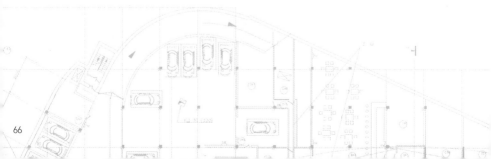

BELOW YOU'LL FIND SOME THOUGHTS AND SUGGESTIONS TO HELP GUIDE YOU IN TALKING ABOUT YOUR NEW LIFE.

DON'T NOT TALK ABOUT IT

Don't keep what's happened in your life to yourself. If you do, you're saying you don't really care about that individual who most needs what Christ has given you. Psalm 40:9 says, **"I proclaim righteousness in the great assembly; I do not seal my lips."** (Pretty good advice if you ask me.)

KEEP IT PERSONAL

Make no mistake: the NEW life you have (and want for others) is all about God. But people are drawn to *your* story of God's intersection with *your* life. People need to hear the answers Jesus offers to them. One of the best ways to get people listening is to talk about the difference Jesus has made in you. *Personally.*

KNOWLEDGE IS YOUR FRIEND

The more you know God through engaging with Him in the Bible, the more effectively you'll be able to speak about the change He's made in your life. Your words will be His Word. You can't share what you don't know. Know God through the Bible.

YOU'RE NOT AN EXPERT

Knowledge is vital. But keeping quiet because you're scared you don't have all the answers is lame. *You're no expert.* No one expects you to be. Often the transparency of saying, "I don't know," will open doors that otherwise might've stayed shut.

BE NICE

Seriously. Just be nice. Don't be a pushover, but don't be a jerk, either. I've yet to see anyone "argued" into the Kingdom of God. The Apostle Paul was excellent at tailoring His approach to meet the needs of different people. It's a good practice for us as well.

YOU'RE NOT ALONE

You have the Holy Spirit inside you! Jesus said the Spirit works to remind you of the things you know (John 14:26), and that He will give you words when you need them (Luke 12:11-2). *See?* You're not alone. Be brave. God is with you. These are just a few thoughts that will hopefully help you as you begin to talk about the change Christ had brought about in your life.

"I have been crucified with Christ and I no longer live, but Christ lives in me. The life I live in the body, I live by faith in the Son of God, who loved me and gave himself for me." Galatians 2:20

A NEW Perspective . . . "

WEEK 4 PREVIEW

This is it . . . the last week in this four-week look at the first steps of your NEW life in Christ.

By this point you should have a good idea about exactly what it means to live this new life. You should have a great understanding of who God is and why it's vital that you continue to grow in your knowledge of Him. And you should know Jesus and why His sacrifice on your behalf was so amazing. You have a really solid base to begin building this NEW life on.

This week you'll look at the final strokes of the picture this book paints. You'll look at a snapshot of what it's like to actually live this NEW life in Christ. You'll be challenged with some very practical actions and attitudes you should begin to take ownership of. And in the end, you'll realize that this life was the one you were always intended to live.

WE'RE CLOSE TO THE END. LET'S GET GOING . . .

HERE'S A LOOK AT WHAT TO EXPECT THIS WEEK:

Week 4, Day 1: A devotion on being salt and light
Week 4, Day 2: A Bible study on embracing humility
Week 4, Day 3: What it means to love the "least of these"
Week 4, Day 4: Living out the Greatest Commandment
Week 4, Day 5: Understanding the tough part of the NEW life
Week 4, Day 6: Seeing the fruit of the Holy Spirit in you

WEEK 4, DAY 1

I said on the previous pages that this week would be all about living the NEW life you have in Christ. We're going to kick off this week with a passage that does a great job of summing up the *reason* behind living this NEW life.

Take a second and read Matthew 5:13-16. This comes at the end of what is called the Sermon on the Mount. The Sermon on the Mount was where Jesus taught His disciples, and a lot of other folks, about the ways of God's Kingdom. It was incredible stuff! Jesus completely flipped what people thought they knew about their faith. It's an amazing sermon and is at the heart of what a NEW life in Christ looks like.

Jesus said some stuff that might need to be looked at a little closer. *First, he said His followers were to be salt.* Most people agree that Jesus could have been referring to a few things: salt's ability to add flavor to substances; salt's ability to preserve food, such as fish; and the belief during this time period that salt was the purest of substances. Make sense? Hold on to your thoughts for a moment.

Jesus said His followers were also to be light. At the most basic level, light drives away darkness. It doesn't take a lot of light to brighten up a dark room. Got it? Again, hold your thoughts.

Jesus completed this thought in verse 16 by giving the reason why it's important that we stand out in this world: *it's not to draw glory or credit to us, but to God.* The idea is that your Christ-like actions will get people's attention. They'll want to know what makes you so different. And you will have the wonderful chance to simply answer them: Christ in me!

Pretty cool, huh?

ANSWER THE FOLLOWING QUESTIONS.

1. Think about your world. How can you be "salt" in how you make a Christ-flavored impact on the world around you?

2. What are some examples of how you can have a preservative effect? In other words, salt keeps food from dying and decaying. How can you be like salt to a world dying apart from God?

3. Give some examples in your daily life where you can be an influence for overall purity? How can you be a "pure substance," like salt, to the world around you?

4. If you had to list one place in your world that needs the light of Christ to drive away the darkness of sin and hopelesness, what would that place be?

WEEK 4, DAY 2

Living as a NEW creation in Christ means your life will grow to look more and more like Jesus' life. **This will take shape in a variety of ways.** In his letter to the Philippians, the Apostle Paul explained how one of these ways looks. Take a second to read Philippians 2:3-11 and then answer the questions below.

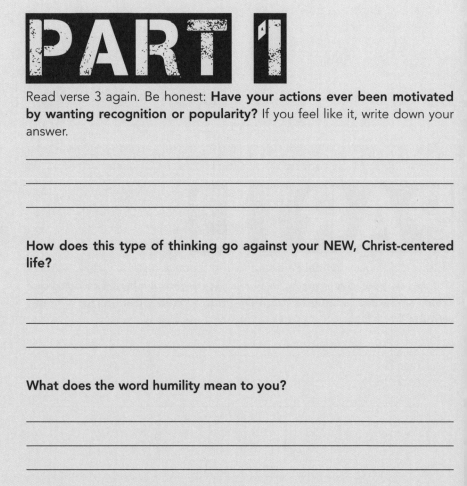

PART 1

Read verse 3 again. Be honest: **Have your actions ever been motivated by wanting recognition or popularity?** If you feel like it, write down your answer.

_____

_____

_____

How does this type of thinking go against your NEW, Christ-centered life?

_____

_____

_____

What does the word humility mean to you?

_____

_____

_____

Re-read verse 4. In the spaces below, write down the name of three people in your life whose needs you could look after in the next few days. For each of them, come up with one specific thing you can do, then commit to doing it!

Read verse 5 again. **Whoa!** Paul said your attitude should be just like Christ's attitude. **In your own words, how do you define a Christ-like attitude? What are some examples of how your attitude can mirror Christ's attitude?**

1. _____

2. _____

3. _____

One of the ways we live this NEW life is in how we care for others. *Especially those who are in most need of our help.* God has some very specific words regarding our attitude toward the poor and needy. Read these words. Spend some time thinking about your attitude toward the poor. **Does it reflect a NEW life in Christ?**

"THEN THE RIGHTEOUS WILL ANSWER HIM, 'LORD, WHEN DID WE SEE YOU HUNGRY AND FEED YOU, OR THIRSTY AND GIVE YOU SOMETHING TO DRINK?" ... "THE KING WILL REPLY, 'I TELL YOU THE TRUTH, WHATEVER YOU DID FOR ONE OF **THE LEAST OF THESE** BROTHERS OF MINE, YOU DID FOR ME." MATTHEW 25:37, 40

"IF THERE IS A **POOR** MAN AMONG YOUR BROTHERS IN ANY OF THE TOWNS OF THE LAND THAT THE LORD YOUR GOD IS GIVING YOU, DO NOT BE HARDHEARTED OR TIGHTFISTED TOWARD YOUR **POOR** BROTHER." DEUTERONOMY 15:7

"RELIGION THAT GOD OUR FATHER ACCEPTS AS PURE AND FAULTLESS IS THIS: TO LOOK AFTER **ORPHANS** AND WIDOWS IN THEIR DISTRESS AND TO KEEP ONESELF FROM BEING POLLUTED BY THE WORLD." JAMES 1:27

WEEK 4, DAY 4

Read Matthew 22:34-40. These guys you just read about were the leaders of the most powerful Jewish religious groups: the Sadducees and the Pharisees. They didn't believe Jesus was the Son of God, and they constantly tried to silence Him. (They ultimately succeeded. These were the guys who arranged Jesus' trial and crucifixion. Of course, their success only lasted three days!) **Part of how they did this was to try and trick Jesus into incorrectly answering questions in front of others.**

In the passage you just read, the Pharisees and Sadducees were trying to trip up Jesus on His interpretation of the Old Testament Law. *Except that Jesus wasn't really in the business of getting tripped up by a bunch of hateful religious dudes.* So, Jesus answered them in a way that was pretty much perfect.

Sum up Jesus' answer here. What are the two things Jesus said to do?

Now, on the following page, you'll have the opportunity to think about how you can begin to **LOVE GOD** and **LOVE PEOPLE**.

In the space provided on the next page, you'll notice a few different categories. For the circles marked "Inward" and "Outward" think about ways you can demonstrate your love for God, both in your own internal thoughts and feelings, and in your outward actions. For the other categories, think of how you might show God's love to the various people represented.

And don't just think about today, think about the future.

INWARD

FRIENDS

FAMILY

OUTWARD

ACQUAINTANCES

WEEK 4, DAY 5

Today you're going to think about something that's not a lot of fun to think about. But it's important, so let's dig right in. Let's start with Jesus' words in John 15:18:

"If the world hates you, keep in mind that it hated me first."

Jesus was talking to His disciples. He was nearing the time in His life where He would be arrested, tried, and murdered. And true to His character, Jesus was still teaching His disciples, right up to the very end.

Jesus said, *"if the world hates you . . ."* But, if you live your life as a Christ-follower, the world *will* hate you. By "the world" I'm talking about those people who reject God and His ways. And by "hate" I mean that they will pretty much be against you and what you stand for.

What are some examples of how the world shows "hatred" for Christ-followers? **In the space provided, write down a few ways you've seen those who don't believe in God really act out against those who do.**

READ THESE WORDS FROM JOHN 15:19.

"If you belonged to the world, it would love you as its own. As it is, you do not belong to the world, but I have chosen you out of the world. That is why the world hates you."

Jesus has chosen *you* to be His. (Wow!) Because of this, you look like Him, not like the world. And the longer you hang out with Jesus, you'll look more and more like Him.

ANSWER THIS: WHY DOES THE WORLD HATE YOU JUST BECAUSE YOU BELONG TO JESUS?

In your opinion, why does it matter? Why couldn't they just leave you and other Christ-followers alone? (Jesus gives one answer to this question in John 15:21, if you want to look there.)

It stinks to think that some people will hate you just because you stand up for what you believe. It isn't easy. But Jesus offers you hope.

LOOK AT WHAT HE SAID IN JOHN 16:33:

"I have told you these things, so that in me you may have peace. In this world you will have trouble. But take heart! I have overcome the world."

All the drama the world is going to bring your way, Jesus says, "Don't worry . . . you have peace in me." Jesus overcame the world! He took the world's best shot (persecution, arrest, and crucifixion) and rose above it (came back to life on the 3rd day)!

In the space below, write down how this makes you feel and how it gives you strength to stand up to the shots the world is going to take at you. Consider writing a short prayer to Jesus expressing these feelings to Him.

WEEK 4, DAY 6

Living the life of a Christ-follower isn't easy. But here's the cool thing: You're not alone. The Holy Spirit lives in you and works to make you more like Christ the longer you follow Christ.

Read Galatians 5:16-26. Verses 16-18 talk about the difference between a life controlled by the Holy Spirit and a life controlled by your sinful nature. In verses 19-21, Paul paints a picture of what living apart from God looks like. But in verses 22-26, Paul shows what it looks like when the Spirit is in charge. *These nine traits are called the "fruit of the Spirit."* Not so much "fruit" like an apple. But *fruit* like "results."

The presence of these nine traits in your life is the result of the Spirit working in you. Somewhere beside the above icons, write down which "fruit" the icon represents. Then, circle one or two that you could really use the Spirit's help with this week. Pray and ask God to remind you to listen to the Spirit showing you how you can be more loving, or peaceful (or whatever) in the week ahead.

WEEK 4 ROUND UP

The goal of this final week was to help you begin to see what it looks like to actively live your NEW life in Christ. Of course, these few snapshots are only the beginning. As you grow in your knowledge of God, you'll learn more and more about what it means to put your faith in action. *As you do, here are two important things to remember . . .*

First, your actions don't make God love you more or less. You're good in God's eyes not because of what you do, but because of what Christ already did. Your motivation for living a Christ-like life should be because you love Jesus. Period.

Secondly, you're not alone! (I can't say this enough.) You don't have to rely on your own strength to live like Christ. The Holy Spirit lives within you, empowering you to live as an imitator of God. And that's pretty cool.

And with these words, the first part of this book has come to a close. But there's plenty more in store for you, both in this book and in your future with Christ.

WHAT NOW?

If you're reading this, chances are you've finished the main part of this little book.

What did you think?

Did you enjoy it? Did it challenge you? Did it help you begin to build a foundation for what this NEW life is all about?

I sincerely pray that it did.

If you found the book helpful, you may be saying to yourself, "What now? What do I do now that I'm done with this?"

Before I answer, I want to let you in on a secret. When we adults try to explain the Gospel to teenagers, we can sometimes muddy it up. *Because we care so much and want to see teenagers discover Christ, we can get ahead of ourselves. We can make it confusing and messy.* A lot of times we make the Gospel 100% about the life after this one. **We tend to make salvation about heaven, and only heaven.** Don't get me wrong! Eternal life with God is a HUGE part of salvation. But it's not the only part.

You see, Jesus lived and died and rose from the dead to give you a vibrant, purpose-filled, amazingly colorful life here on this earth. Right now. Today.

He made you who you are. He put you in your town, in this span of history, among the people you find yourself interacting with daily. He didn't do this by accident. He did it so you'd have an amazing impact on your world, in His name.

"What now?" you ask. I'll answer you: Don't wait. Live your life on mission with God. And live it now! The NEW life you've discovered in Christ is the secret to the most fulfilling life you can imagine. Don't miss it.

MORE NEW STUFF FOR THE NEW YOU

The main idea behind NEW was to help you grasp some of the basics of your new relationship with God. But we wanted to do something more for you. We wanted to help provide you with some information that would allow you to go a little deeper in how you understand God and how you continue to live a life that imitates Christ's life.

IN THIS NEXT SECTION YOU'LL FIND SOME CHARTS, SOME LISTS . . . REALLY, YOU'LL FIND A LOT OF COOL STUFF.

Some of it will help you immediately. Some you may find useful down the road. But all of the content in this last section is designed to help give you some handles on how to begin to own your faith more and more. So, check them out! And be sure to refer back to them when you need them.

MORE NEW STUFF

WHAT YOU NEED TO KNOW ABOUT THE BOOKS OF THE BIBLE

OLD TESTAMENT

Genesis	Joshua	Job	Isaiah
Exodus	Judges	Psalms	Jeremiah
Leviticus	Ruth	Proverbs	Lamentations
Numbers	1 Samuel	Ecclesiastes	Ezekiel
Deuteronomy	2 Samuel	Song of Solomon	Daniel
	1 Kings		
	2 Kings		
	1 Chronicles		
	2 Chronicles		
	Ezra		
	Nehemiah		
	Esther		

NEW TESTAMENT

Matthew	Acts	Romans	Hebrews
Mark		1 Corinthians	James
Luke		2 Corinthians	1 Peter
John		Galatians	2 Peter
		Ephesians	1 John
		Philippians	2 John
		Colossians	3 John
		1 Thessalonians	Jude
		2 Thessalonians	
		1 Timothy	
		2 Timothy	
		Titus	
		Philemon	

Hosea
Joel
Amos
Obadiah
Jonah
Micah
Nahum
Habakkuk
Zephaniah
Haggai
Zechariah
Malachi

Revelation

The Bible is the story of how God has rescued, is rescuing, and will rescue His people! You probably know it's made up of different unique sections called "books." The different Books of the Bible are laid out in chronological order (mostly, though there are a few exceptions) from Genesis to Revelation.

While all Scripture is God-inspired, all Scripture isn't exactly the same. What do I mean? Well, there are different types of books, which explains how some books seem so different than others.

On these pages, you'll see the Books of the Bible laid out in the order they appear in Scripture, divided by the Old Testament and the New Testament. You'll notice that each Book is shaded to show the specific type of literature it represents. Refer to the key below as a guide

OLD TESTAMENT BOOKS

Law   History

Poetry   Major Prophets

Minor Prophets

NEW TESTAMENT BOOKS

Gospel   History

Paul's Letters General Letters

Prophecy

THE BIBLE TIMELINE: WHEN IT ALL HAPPENED

STUFF THAT HAPPENED IN THE OLD TESTAMENT

??? | 2200 BC | 1800 | 1200 | 900

- God creates everything
- Adam & Eve
- Sin enters the picture
- Noah & The Flood

- Israelites enslaved in Egypt
- Moses called to lead them out!
- The Exodus happens
- After lots of walking, Israelites enter Promised Land

- Israel splits into two Kingdoms
- Downfall is coming!

- Abraham makes covenant with God
- Isaac is born
- Jacob is on the scene
- Joseph doing his thing in Egypt

- Period of the Judges
- Samuel on the scene
- Saul chosen as King
- David anointed as TRUE King
- Solomon is King. Israel at height of power.

STUFF THAT HAPPENED IN THE NEW TESTAMENT

0 | 20 AD | 30 | 40 | 50

- Jesus is born. Which is awesome.

- John the Baptist on the scene
- Jesus baptized, beginning of ministry
- Jesus calls disciples
- Jesus teaches, heals, does miracles
- Last Supper
- Jesus' arrest, death, and resurrection

- Paul's 1st Missionary Journey
- Paul's 2nd Missionary Journey
- Paul meets Timothy

- Paul's 3rd Missionary Journey
- Paul visits with Ephesian elders
- Goes to Jerusalem against their wishes

- Holy Spirit comes at Pentecost
- Jerusalem Church grows strong
- Stephen is martyred
- Jerusalem church faces fierce persecution. Scatters.
- Paul converted

One of the most important things to know as you lay the foundation for your NEW life with Christ is the basic flow of the Bible. *In other words, it's good to know what happened when.* This chart is a super simple version of a biblical timeline. The dates aren't exact, but they're close! **The idea is to simply give you an overview of the big picture story of the Bible.**

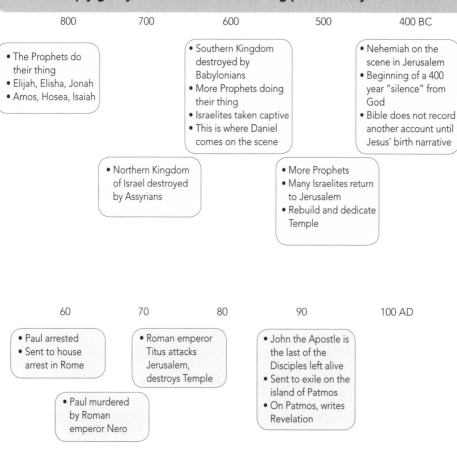

800   700   600   500   400 BC

- The Prophets do their thing
- Elijah, Elisha, Jonah
- Amos, Hosea, Isaiah

- Southern Kingdom destroyed by Babylonians
- More Prophets doing their thing
- Israelites taken captive
- This is where Daniel comes on the scene

- Nehemiah on the scene in Jerusalem
- Beginning of a 400 year "silence" from God
- Bible does not record another account until Jesus' birth narrative

- Northern Kingdom of Israel destroyed by Assyrians

- More Prophets
- Many Israelites return to Jerusalem
- Rebuild and dedicate Temple

60   70   80   90   100 AD

- Paul arrested
- Sent to house arrest in Rome

- Roman emperor Titus attacks Jerusalem, destroys Temple

- John the Apostle is the last of the Disciples left alive
- Sent to exile on the island of Patmos
- On Patmos, writes Revelation

- Paul murdered by Roman emperor Nero

BIBLE VERSES BY TOPIC: IN CASE YOU WERE WONDERING

HERE'S WHAT THE BIBLE SAYS ABOUT . . .

Access to God
Psalm 145:18, John 14:16, Ephesians 3:12, 1 Peter 3:18

Being Generous
Proverbs 11:24, Proverbs 19:17, Matthew 10:42, Acts 20:35

Being Honest
Proverbs 4:25-27, Proverbs 12:2, Luke 6:31, 2 Corinthians 4:1-2

Being Humble
Matthew 5:3, Matthew 23:12, Mark 10:45, Romans 12:10, 1 Peter 5:5

Being Kind
Matthew 5:7, Ephesians 4:32, 1 Peter 3:8-9, 1 John 3:18

Feeling Angry
Proverbs 15:18, Proverbs 22:4, Romans 12:19, James 1:19

Feeling Nervous or Anxious
Isaiah 41:10, Matthew 6:33-34, Philippians 4:6-7, Philippians 4:13

Feeling Sad
Psalm 55:22, Psalm 121:1-2, Isaiah 66:13, Matthew 5:4

Feeling Scared
Psalm 23:1-4, Psalm 34:4, 2 Corinthians 12:10, John 14:27

Forgiveness
Psalm 103:8-12, Matthew 6:14, 2 Corinthians 5:18-19, Ephesians 1:7-10

Friendship
Proverbs 13:20, Proverbs 17:17, Proverbs 27:17, Romans 12:10,
1 Corinthians 15:33

God's Faithfulness
Psalm 33:4, Psalm 36:5, Matthew 24:35, 1 Corinthians 1:9

God's Glory
Psalm 19:1-4, Psalm 57:5, Psalm 96:3, Revelation 4:11

We wanted to give you a quick reference of how the Bible deals with key themes. Use this list as a starting point when you need to seek out God on any of these issues. But just know this: the Bible doesn't address every issue you'll deal with in this life "by name." (For example, you won't find the phrase "Internet Pornography" in the Bible.) But, you can be confident that the Bible does address the heart of every issue you'll encounter. (And so you'll find a lot of references to holiness and purity when it comes to sex and sexuality.)

God's Grace
Romans 3:20-24, Romans 5:1-2, Ephesians 2:4-9, 1 Peter 4:10

God's Love
Psalm 42:8, Psalm 103:13, John 3:16, Romans 5:8, 1 John 3:1, 1 John 4:16

God's Power
Isaiah 26:4, Jeremiah 10:12, Matthew 19:26, 1 Peter 5:6

Gossip
Proverbs 16:28, Luke 6:45, Ephesians 4:29-32, Matthew 5:11

Heaven
John 3:36, John 14:2, Acts 4:12, Philippians 3:20-21, Revelation 21:4

Joy
Psalm 5:11-12, Psalm 9:2, John 16:33, Philippians 4:4

Living A Christ-like Life
Matthew 5:13-16, 1 Corinthians 10:31, Colossians 1:10, 1 Peter 2:12

Needing Some Encouragement
Deuteronomy 31:6, Psalm 9:9, John 16:33, 2 Corinthians 4:16-18

Obedience
Psalm 25:10, Matthew 5:19, John 14:15, 1 John 2:3-6

Sex and Sexuality
Matthew 5:27-30, 1 Corinthians 6:18, Ephesians 5:3, 1 Thessalonians 4:1-8, Hebrews 13:4

Tough Times
Psalm 91:1-2, Proverbs 3:5-6, Matthew 11:28-30, 1 Peter 1:6-9

[SOME OF] THE PEOPLE OF THE BIBLE

ABRAHAM–*Father of the Israelites, God's chosen people*
• **Main Passage:** Genesis 11-25. **Other Places:** Exodus 2:24; Matthew 1:1, 2; Luke 3:34; Acts 7:2-8; Romans 4; Galatians 3; Hebrews 2; 6-7; 11.

ADAM–*First guy. Ever. Got to hang out with God before his sin caused God to send him out of the Garden.*
• **Main Passage:** Genesis 1:26-5:5. **Other Places:** Luke 3:38; Romans 5:14; 1 Corinthians 15:22, 45; 1 Timothy 2:13-14

DAVID–*Shepherd boy turned mighty king. God called David a man after His own heart. Wrote most of Psalms.*
• **Main Passage:** 1 Samuel 16-1 Kings 2. **Other Places:** Matthew 1:1-6; 22:43-45; Luke 1:32; Acts 13:22; Romans 1:3; Hebrews 11:32

ELIJAH–*Second most famous of Israel's prophets. Defeated prophets of Baal. Landed on the bad side of King Ahab and Queen Jezebel.*
• **Main Passage:** 1 Kings 17:1-2 Kings 2:11. **Other Places:** Matthew 11:14; 16:14; 17:3-13; 27:47-49; Luke 1:17; 4:25-26; Romans 11:2-4; James 5:17-18

EVE–*First girl. Ever. Got to hang out with God before her sin caused God to send her out of the Garden.*
• **Main Passage:** Genesis 2:18-4:26

ISAAC–*Son of the covenant born to Abraham and Sarah. Dad to Jacob and Esau.*
• **Main Passage:** Genesis 17:15-35:29. **Other Places:** Romans 9:7-10; Hebrews 11:17-20; James 2:21

ISAIAH–*Greatest Old Testament prophet*
• **Main Passage:** 2 Kings 19:2-20:19. **Other Places:** Matthew 3:3; 8:17; 12:17-21; John 12:38-41; Romans 10:16-21

JACOB–*Grandson of Abraham. Son of Isaac. Father of the 12 Tribes of Israel. Flawed dude, but still used by God.*
• **Main Passage:** Genesis 25-50. **Other Places:** Matthew 1:2; 22:32; Acts 7:8-16; Romans 9:11-13; Hebrews 11:9, 20-21

JOHN THE BAPTIST–*Jesus' cousin. Prophet called by God to prepare the way for Jesus.*
• **Main Passage:** All four Gospels. **Other Places:** Isaiah 40:3, Malachi 4:5; Acts 1:5, 22; 11:16; 13:25; 18:25; 19:3-4

JOHN THE APOSTLE–*Called the "beloved disciple." Wrote Gospel of John, 1, 2, 3 John, and Revelation.*
• **Main Passage:** All four Gospels, Acts, and Revelation.

The Bible is full of amazing narratives of REAL people. When you look deeper into their lives, you realize most of them are like us: they get it right sometimes, and other times they blow it. **These are just a few of the major characters in the Bible.**

JOSEPH—*Amazing story! Sold into slavery by his brothers. Falsely imprisoned. Became great Egyptian ruler.*
• **Main Passage:** Genesis 30-50. **Other Places:** Hebrews 11:22

JOSHUA—*Powerful leader of Israel. Took over for Moses. Led Israelites into Promised Land.*
• **Main Passage:** Book of Joshua. **Other Places:** Exodus 17:9-14; 24:13; 33:11; Numbers 27:18-23; 32:11-12; Deuteronomy 3:28; 31:7, 14; Judges 2:6-9

MARY, MOTHER OF JESUS—*Jesus' virgin mother. God miraculously formed Jesus in her womb.*
• **Main Passage:** All four Gospels. **Other Places:** Acts 1:14

MOSES—*Author of first five Books of the Bible. God's chosen deliverer of Israelites from Egyptian slavery. Sin kept him from entering the Promised Land. But faithful leader of God's people.*
• **Main Passage:** Exodus through Deuteronomy. **Other Places:** Acts 7:20-44; Hebrews 11:23-29

NOAH—*Chosen along with his family to live through the Flood. 2nd father of all people. Not perfect, but faithful.*
• **Main Passage:** Genesis 5:28-10:32. **Other Places:** Isaiah 54:9; Hebrews 11:7; 1 Peter 3:20

PAUL—*Outside of Christ, most influential person for Christianity. Converted persecutor of Christ-followers. Wrote 13 New Testament Books.*
• **Main Passage:** Acts 7:58-28:31. **Other Places:** See all his letters.

PETER—*Unofficial leader of the disciples. Impetuous but passionate. Denied Christ but was forgiven by the resurrected Jesus. Delivered sermon at Pentecost. Prominent New Testament leader.*
• **Main Passage:** All four Gospels and Book of Acts. **Other Places:** Galatians 1:18, 2:7-14; 1, 2 Peter

RAHAB—*Prostitute who came to believe in God. Rescued Joshua and Caleb. Included in Jesus' lineage.*
• **Main Passage:** Joshua 2, 6:22-23. **Other Places:** Matthew 1:5; Hebrews 11:31; James 2:25

RUTH—*Faithful daughter-in-law to Naomi. Wife to Boaz. Great-grandmother to David.*
• **Main Passage:** Book of Ruth. **Other Places:** Matthew 1:5

TIMOTHY—*Mentored by Paul. Young pastor and leader in the New Testament Church. Recipient of Paul's letters 1 and 2 Timothy.*
• **Main Passage:** Acts 16. **Other Places:** 1 Corinthians 4:17; 16:10-11; Philippians 2:19-23; 1 Thessalonians 3:2-6; Hebrews 13:23

THE STORY THROUGH STORIES

CREATION
God makes all things.
Genesis 1-2

GOD CREATES HUMANS. HUMANS FAIL GOD.
Adam and Eve's sin created a barrier between humans and God.
Genesis 3

GOD CALLS A PEOPLE AS HIS OWN
In spite of their sin, God called the Israelites.
Genesis 12, 13, 15, 17

GOD'S PEOPLE ENSLAVED
The Israelites = slaves in Egypt for 400 years
Exodus 1

GOD'S PEOPLE FREED
God delivered His people. Promised a land of their own.
Exodus, Leviticus, Numbers, Deuteronomy, Joshua

GOD'S PEOPLE ESTABLISHED
God's people entered the Promised Land.
Joshua

GOD'S PEOPLE SOAR
Under David and Solomon, Israel = wealthy, powerful nation
1 and 2 Samuel, 1 Kings 10:29, 1 Chronicles-2 Chronicles 9:30

We can make the Bible about a lot of things. In its simplest form, the Bible is a story. *THE story.* It's the story of God's plan to rescue humans from sin. The cool thing? You can follow the big picture story of God's plan through a series of shorter stories. When you get a chance, trace the story of God's rescue plan through these individual stories.

GOD'S PEOPLE FALL
God gave His people lots of warning. But the Israelites rebelled against God and He allowed their destruction.
1 Kings 11-2 Kings, 2 Chronicles 10-36

GOD'S RESCUE MISSION FORETOLD
God sent word of a once-and-for-all hero who would rescue God's people from sin.
Isaiah 9:6, Isaiah 53:5-12, Micah 5:2

GOD'S PLAN FOR RESCUE BEGINS
Jesus, the Messiah, the Son of God, came to earth. Fully God, fully man.
Luke 2

GOD'S RESCUE MISSION COMES TO LIFE
Jesus lived, taught, healed, and performed miracles for three years.
The Gospels

JESUS GUARANTEES OUR RESCUE
Jesus' obedient death on the cross once and for all destroyed the barrier of sin.
Matthew 27, Mark 15, Luke 23, John 18-19

THE RESCUE MISSION LIVED OUT
Full of the Holy Spirit, the New Testament believers spread their faith all over the world.
Acts, Paul's Letters, General Letters

THE RESCUE MISSION COMPLETE
God sent John the Apostle a vision of what the future would hold. God will usher in a new creation. A perfect one. We will be with Him forever.
Revelation

NEXT STEPS FOR GROWING CHRIST-FOLLOWERS

By this point you've figured out that *NEW* is designed for, well, new Christ-followers. But, since growing in your faith is a huge part of following Christ, we couldn't resist giving you this little section where we offer some strategies to help you move forward as a Christ-follower.

Over the next few pages, you'll find several different sections containing ideas for ways you can continue to grow in your faith. These are basically practices that help you know God more and better. So, while you're going to see a collection of "stuff to do," the goal is actually a deeper relationship with God.

As you're ready, consider choosing some of the following practices to engage in.

A LIFE OF PRAYER

While we gave you a basic model of how to pray on page 48, there are quite a variety of ways of approaching God in prayer. Here are a few suggestions.

Prayer Journal
- Prayer journals are an awesome way to track specific prayers (so you can go back and see how God answered them), keep up with people you know need prayer, and to organize how you pray for the various needs in your life and in the lives of others. Go old school or digital, whatever suits you best. Consider organizing your journal a few different ways:
    - o Maybe you have sections for family, personal, friends, and so on.
    - o Or maybe you have sections for prayers answered, or "praises," where you record where God answered a prayer.
    - o However you organize it, keeping a prayer journal helps keep you consistent. It's an awesome way to track how God is moving in your life and in the lives of others.

Fasting
- Fasting is where you sacrifice food for a defined (and usually limited) period of time in order to concentrate on God or a specific spiritual issue.
    - o When your mind turns to your desire to eat, it reminds you to pray or meditate on Scripture, or listen to God.
- In Matthew 6 Jesus warns that fasting should be a private matter, never done in public to show off, or to appear super-religious. Fasting is between you and God, though it's OK for your parents or youth pastor to know.
    - o [**Note:** Fasting should never be done for an extended period of time. Most people fast for one day, usually not eating from the time they wake up until they eat supper. It's important to drink fluids, as well. God doesn't desire for you to put your body in danger or stress just to draw closer to Him. It's probably best not to try fasting until you talk to an adult.]

Intercessory Prayer
- Intercessory prayer is a fancy phrase for praying for others. It sounds simple, but it is a powerful aspect of your prayer life.
    - o Not only does God hear our prayers on behalf of others, it has the cool effect of making us more compassionate to what's going on in other people's lives.

A LIFE IN THE WORD
There are different ways to engage God in Scripture in addition to the model we gave you on page 30. Here are a few of them.

Discovering Jesus
- Simply, this is you committing to reading a Gospel all the way through. (Many people start with Mark.) The idea is to read through an entire book looking for what Jesus said, what He did, what He valued, what He says about life . . . and to think about your life and how He speaks to you.

Book Studies
- Easy as it sounds. Simply choosing a Book of the Bible and reading it all the way through. There are a ton of resources available Online and at bookstores that can help guide you. Ask your youth minister or pastor to recommend one.

Scripture Memorization

- Psalm 119 talks about the benefits of hiding God's Word in your heart. This happens through memorizing Scripture. There are a lot of different lists of vital verses for memorizing Online, as well as tools to help you memorize them. Knowing God's Word by heart is essential for Christ-followers.

Theme or Topic Studies

- This is a fun way to read Scripture. Choose a topic such as love, or forgiveness, or jealousy, or whatever, and trace it through Scripture to see all the different ways the Bible addresses it.
  - o To do this, you could start with the concordance in the back of a printed Bible.
  - o You could also use the search function on your Bible app, or go to any one of the great Bible search engines Online.
  - o (My favorite is biblegateway.com. It's easy to use and there are a lot of tools.)

Engaging Your Doubts

- As you grow in your faith, you'll have questions about spiritual issues. Instead of ignoring them or trying to bury them, engage with them! Using the resources available to you in your Bible and Online, go as deep as you can in studying any questions you have.
  - o Make it your mission to leave no stone unturned.
  - o God is faithful! He'll meet you in your search, you can be sure of that!

A LIFE THAT SACRIFICES

Sacrificing for others in the name of Jesus is a big part of being a follower of Christ. Jesus said it Himself, "The greatest among you will be your servant" (Matt. 23:11).

Sacrificial Giving
- Do you have a job? Do you get an allowance? If you can answer "yes" to either of these, you're in a great position to start giving back from what God has blessed you with. Financial giving starts with the realization that Jesus is the giver of all things. You have money because He's blessed you or your parents with the ability to earn money. Giving sacrificially means giving God a portion of your money as a way of saying thanks.
    - o A good starting point is 10% of what you receive. (You might hear this called a "tithe.")
    - o You can give to your church or to another ministry. The important thing is that it's done willingly and thankfully.

Service
- The giving of your time and energy in service to another is one of the greatest demonstrations of being a Christ-follower. When you go on a mission trip, or volunteer at the local food pantry, or any other volunteer organization, you're showing the world that you're unselfish with your time and gifts.
    - o God honors this type of selfless sacrifice. It's an amazing way to draw closer to God and to show the world whom you are identified with.

Taking Up A Cause
- Similar to service, taking up a cause is an awesome way to use your time and energy for the greater good. What causes or issues are you passionate about? Human trafficking? Hunger? Girls' rights in developing nations? Identify your passion, and then try to find a Christian organization that's doing a good job of helping in that area. (Get with your parent(s) and look up Charity Navigator Online. It's an awesome site that ranks charities in order of their effectiveness and financial responsibility.)
    - o If you can't find a Christian organization, by all means, look for a secular one.
    - o And if you can't find any organization, start your own!
    - o The point is to get on board with a cause, and to do so as a follower of Christ. Give your time, energy, money, and passion to helping make a difference in this world.

A LIFE OF SALT AND LIGHT

In Matthew 5 Jesus talked about being "salt" and "light." Being "salt" is making an active difference in the world around you. Being "light" is shining the light of Christ into dark places.

Sharing Your Light
- Consider asking your youth minister if you can teach a Bible study some-time. Or share some of what God has been doing in your life in front of your Church or youth group. You have no idea what an encouragement this type of outward communication could be to your friends, or even adults!

Discipling Someone
- As you grow in your faith, you'll have the opportunity to be a strong spiritual influence on your friends. Maybe you'll even get the chance to help some of them in their journey of becoming a disciple of Jesus.
  - o It doesn't mean you're an expert. It just means you're walking with them on this journey, sharing life, encouraging them, and keeping each other accountable to living the Christ-life.

Growing A Community
- This one is a little difficult to do on your own. But, it doesn't mean you can't give it all you've got. Here's a fact: God made us to be in community with each other. We were never meant to live the Christ-life alone. As you grow in your faith, having a solid community of friends who are Christ-followers will be essential. You can be the "glue-person," that guy or girl who holds things together.
  - o Take the challenge to be the one who keeps everyone focused on how great it is to have a group of friends on this discipleship jour-ney together.

ABOUT THE AUTHOR

Andy Blanks is the co-founder and Publisher for ym360. Andy has been designing Bible study and discipleship resources for youth ministers and teen agers since 2003. He lives in Birmingham, AL with wonderful wife Brendt, their three daughters, and son. He's a pretty big fan of both the Boston Red S and anything involving the Auburn Tigers. When h not hanging out with his family or volunteering at church's youth ministry, you can find Andy trail running or mountain biking. Follow him in Instagram: andy_blanks

YM36O BLOG

A Leading Source of Daily Youth Ministry Info and Insight

The ym360 Blog Team of youth ministry veterans and leaders is committed to providing daily content in the following areas:

Bible Stuff: These posts challenge you with biblical principles for your ministry and your students

Training: Covering the "how-to's" of youth ministry, these invaluable articles help you be a better youth worker

Trends & Culture: Stay on top of the latest studies, research, and trends from the world of youth culture

Networking: These posts provide a glimpse of other ministries and individuals doing great youth ministry

Free Stuff: Our way of equipping you with lessons, devotions for students, and much more. . . on the house!

SERVING THOUSANDS OF YOUTH WORKERS

USING SOCIAL MEDIA TO PROVIDE COMMUNITY AND NETWORKING TO THOUSANDS OF YOUTH WORKERS

 Genuine community with thousands of youth workers at www.facebook.com/youthministry360

 Get snippets of trends/culture and more youth ministry info by following @ym360